An Arrow to the Heart

Order this book online at www.trafford.com/07-1288
or email orders@trafford.com

Most Trafford titles are also available at major online book retailers.

© Copyright 2007 Ken McLeod.

All rights reserved. No part of this publication may be reproduced, stored in a retrieval system, or transmitted, in any form or by any means, electronic, mechanical, photocopying, recording, or otherwise, without the written prior permission of the author.

Illustrations © Copyright 2007 Dick Allen
Book and cover design by Deborah Neikirk
Photography by Jeff Bickford & Gail Gustafson
Translation of the *Heart Sutra* by Ken McLeod

Note for Librarians: A cataloguing record for this book is available from Library and Archives Canada at www.collectionscanada.ca/amicus/index-e.html

Printed in Victoria, BC, Canada.

ISBN: 978-1-4251-3377-1

We at Trafford believe that it is the responsibility of us all, as both individuals and corporations, to make choices that are environmentally and socially sound. You, in turn, are supporting this responsible conduct each time you purchase a Trafford book, or make use of our publishing services. To find out how you are helping, please visit www.trafford.com/responsiblepublishing.html

Our mission is to efficiently provide the world's finest, most comprehensive book publishing service, enabling every author to experience success. To find out how to publish your book, your way, and have it available worldwide, visit us online at www.trafford.com/10510

www.trafford.com

North America & international
toll-free: 1 888 232 4444 (USA & Canada)
phone: 250 383 6864 ♦ fax: 250 383 6804
email: info@trafford.com

The United Kingdom & Europe
phone: +44 (0)1865 722 113 ♦ local rate: 0845 230 9601
facsimile: +44 (0)1865 722 868 ♦ email: info.uk@trafford.com

10 9 8 7 6 5 4 3 2

An Arrow to the Heart

A COMMENTARY ON THE HEART SUTRA
BY
KEN MCLEOD

Acknowledgements

Numerous individuals played crucial roles in bringing this book to its present form — Yvonne Rand's consistent encouragement, the keen editorial eye of Janaki Symon and the helpful contributions of Ann Braun, Richard Collins, Lynea Diaz-Hagan, George Draffan, Claudia Hansson, Carolyn Hudson, Scott Lawrance, Sandy Pollock, Ajahn Thanasanti, Jeff Tip, and others. Dick Allen generously provided commentary in the form of the illustrations that complement the text. And I'm grateful to Deborah Neikirk for designing the book and shepherding it through the publication process.

This commentary itself builds on the work of other teachers and scholars, notably Hakuin, Red Pine, and Stephen Batchelor.

Most influential, perhaps, is Hakuin's *Zen Words for the Heart*, a commentary from another age and another culture — 17th century Japanese Zen. No doubt sitting on a pile of wordy and philosophical commentaries, Hakuin took up a sword and slashed — there really is no other word for it — through all conceptual thinking. His combination of prose and poetry cuts away everything and leaves the reader with nothing but the awake knowing the sutra presents.

Red Pine's commentary, *The Heart Sutra: the Womb of Buddhas*, truly shows what depth of scholarship combined with sensitivity to practice can do to illuminate the meaning of a text and to make the subtleties of the teaching accessible.

In *Verses From the Center* Stephen Batchelor interprets Nagarjuna's verses as a precise investigation of experience through the lens of questioning attention. In doing so, Stephen opened the door for other Western teachers to give experiential, rather than academic, interpretations of classical texts.

I was able to write this book only because of the continued support and encouragement from students here in Los Angeles and elsewhere. To all of them I am humbly grateful.

Ken McLeod
Los Angeles, 2007

Introduction

Form is emptiness.
Emptiness is form.
Emptiness is not other than form.
Form is not other than emptiness.

For centuries these four sentences have echoed down the corridors of time. The echoes continue today, wherever the *Heart Sutra* is recited, in Tibetan and Mongolian monasteries, Chinese, Japanese and Korean temples, and, now, in monasteries, temples, and centers all through Europe and North and South America.

Clearly, the *Heart Sutra* is not a devotional work, though it is an object of devotion for many. You find no exhortations to piety, no articles of faith, no inspirational imagery. Nor is it an ethical statement, for it is free from any moral injunctions or guidelines for behavior. If you are looking for the authority of Buddha, you find he says only a single sentence of confirmation — nothing else. It is not a meditation guide, at least, not a very good one, for the few instructions are abstruse and inaccessible. For many people, their first impression is one of overwhelming negation: no this, no that, no that, no this, down, down, down a long list of puzzling terms.

Why, then, is this short text held in such high regard?

The *Heart Sutra* is about the perfection of wisdom — an understanding of life and being that is experiential, not conceptual or intellectual. Just as a description of the taste of a cherry pie provides nothing to satisfy hunger and little to enjoy, a conceptual understanding of the perfection of wisdom does little to change how we actually understand life and live it. As a verse in praise of the perfection of wisdom says:

> *Perfection of Wisdom, inexpressible, inconceivable, indescribable,*
> *Without beginning or end, like the sky itself,*
> *The experience of pristine awareness, knowing itself.*
> *To the mother of the buddhas of the three times, I bow.*

Read the four lines about form and emptiness again, slowly — or say them, slowly. What happens? For a moment, or perhaps a little longer, the incessant cacophony of thoughts, memories, and associations in your head stops. Even the echoes stop. Granted, if you are encountering these words for the first time, that gap probably lasts only a moment and is usually followed by a "Huh?" But your mind does stop. What do you experience, right there? That experience, and what follows from it, is what the *Heart Sutra* is pointing to.

Defying all logic, these four lines reveal a different way of experiencing life, a way in which the usual dualities are not opposites, but complementary expressions of a deeper knowing. That deeper knowing is the subject of the *Heart Sutra*. A commentary to the sutra aims to help the reader or student come closer to that knowing.

Traditionally, teachers in each generation offer their own commentaries to their students, commentaries that bring out points in the texts that are relevant for their time and culture. While hundreds of Asian commentaries have been written on the *Heart Sutra*, commentaries by Western teachers are only now beginning to appear.

In contrast to most commentaries, I approach the *Heart Sutra* not as a philosophical exposition of emptiness, but as the presentation of a moment of being completely awake and present. Any attempt to explain such an experience is pointless and futile. It is beyond explanation. Accordingly, the aim of this commentary is not to explain this experience to you, but to elicit it in you.

On each page, you will find a poetic riff that may evoke an insight or a question, a prose riff that often includes questions for you to consider, and notes that provide information on the technical terms and references sprinkled throughout the text. The commentary proceeds line by line, phrase by phrase, eschewing any attempt to explain the structure or progression of the dialectic.

The commentary is not quite as arbitrary as it may seem. In some sections, I based the poetic and prose riffs on classical exegeses. As an example, consider the line:

> *It is not born or destroyed, impure or free from impurity, not incomplete or complete.*

According to one tradition of interpretation, this line refers to the three marks of existence: impermanence, suffering, and non-self. At the same time Avalokiteshvara is instructing Sharipurta that these marks of existence are not absolutes. He is also saying that such frameworks for interpreting experience don't arise when one is completely present. I have tried to reflect these three levels of understanding in the commentaries on each phrase.

You will probably do best if you begin by reading this book a page or two at a time. You may find that the abrupt shifts in logic and images create gaps in your ordinary thinking. When a gap arises, stay there for a few moments, allowing time for you to see or consider things a little differently. On your first read, don't make any attempt to "understand" the words. Instead, just experience the shifts, and see what you come away with.

Attempts to figure out the underlying structure will just enmesh you in thinking and take you away from the possibility of knowing directly what the *Heart Sutra* is pointing to. Save those for later reads.

Why is emptiness such an important teaching in Mahayana Buddhism? The short answer is that emptiness opens the door to a qualitatively different kind of compassion. Compassion is usually understood as an emotion, but the kind of compassion that Avalokiteshvara represents (it's no coincidence that he delivers the *Heart Sutra*) is compassion as presence. Emptiness frees us from concerns about who we are, what others may think, or what we should or should not do. At the same time, it brings a clarity that enables us to know what to do, moment by moment, to respond to the suffering and struggles of the world.

The Sutra

The Sutra of the Heart of Lady Perfection of Wisdom

I bow to Lady Perfection of Wisdom

Thus have I heard. At one time Lord Buddha was staying at Vulture Peak Mountain in Rajagriha, with a great gathering of the monastic sangha and the bodhisattva sangha.

At that time, Lord Buddha entered an absorption, called *Profound Radiance*, in which all elements of experience are present.

At the same time, noble Avalokiteshvara, the bodhisattva mahasattva, was looking right at the experience of the profound perfection of wisdom and he saw the five groups to be empty of nature.

Then, through the power of the Buddha, venerable Shariputra asked noble Avalokiteshvara, the bodhisattva mahasattva, "How does a son or daughter of the noble family, who wishes to practice the profound perfection of wisdom, train?"

Addressed in this way, noble Avalokiteshvara, the bodhisattva mahasattva, said to venerable Shariputra, "O Shariputra, a son or daughter of the noble family who wishes to practice the profound perfection of wisdom looks in this way: see the five groups to be truly empty of nature.

Form is emptiness; emptiness is form. Emptiness is not other than form; form is not other than emptiness. In the same way, feeling, concept, mental formation, and consciousness are emptiness.

Therefore, Shariputra, all experience is emptiness. It is not defined. It is not born or destroyed, impure or free from impurity, not incomplete or complete.

Therefore, Shariputra, in emptiness, there is no form, no feeling, no concept, no mental formation, no consciousness; no eye, no ear, no nose, no tongue, no body, no mind, no appearance, no sound, no smell, no taste, no touch, no mind object; no eye element up to no mind element and no mind consciousness element; no ignorance, no end of ignorance up to no old age and death, no end of old age and death; no suffering, no origin, no cessation, no path; no pristine awareness, no attainment, and no non-attainment.

Therefore, Shariputra, because, for bodhisattvas, there is no attainment, they rest, trusting the perfection of wisdom. With nothing clouding their minds, they have no fear. They leave delusion behind and come to the end of nirvana.

All the buddhas of the three times, by trusting this perfection of wisdom, fully awaken in unsurpassable, true, complete awakening.

Therefore, the mantra of the perfection of wisdom, the mantra of great awareness, the unsurpassed mantra, the mantra equal to the unequalled, the mantra that completely calms all suffering is not a ruse: know it to be true.

Thus, the mantra of the perfection of wisdom is said in this way:

om gaté gaté paragaté parasamgaté bodhi svaha

Thus, Shariputra, do all bodhisattva mahasattvas train in the profound perfection of wisdom."

Then Lord Buddha arose from that absorption and praised noble Avalokiteshvara, the bodhisattva mahasattva, saying, "Well done, well done, o son of noble family; thus it is, thus it is. One practices the profound perfection of wisdom just as you have taught. Those Who Have Gone This Way also rejoice."

Then venerable Shariputra and noble Avalokiteshvara, the bodhisattva mahasattva, that whole assembly and the world with its gods, humans, titans, and sky spirits, rejoiced and praised the words of Lord Buddha.

The Title

The Sutra of the Heart of Lady Perfection of Wisdom

What's in a name? That which we call a rose
By any other name would smell as sweet.
 — William Shakespeare, *Romeo and Juliet*

Sutra

You take a seat and
  your eyes meet.
Question, answer,
  weave together.
Inside, outside
  fade away.
"That's it," echoes
  in timeless space.

You leave.

Everything and nothing have changed.

You are forever lost now.
  That's how it goes.

Sutra, suture? — let's just say it holds things together. The Tibetans chose *mdo* (they pronounce it *doh*), a crossroads, where things meet.

This meeting? It's a mystery... You know something took place, but you can't put it in words.

No one can.

That's why they call it a transmission outside the sutras.

You look at your world — friends, family, home, work, and play. Everything's there, just as before... and yet, not just as before.

No longer at ease in the old dispensation, now what do you do?

Notes

Sutra, suture
The two words have the common etymological root *to sew* (the Sanskrit *sivyati* and the Latin *suere*).

where things meet
The teacher's mind and the student's

a transmission outside the sutras
A phrase used in both the Dzogchen and Zen traditions. Similar phrasing is found in the Sufi and other awareness-based traditions.

at ease in the old dispensation
> We returned to our places, these Kingdoms,
> But no longer at ease here, in the old dispensation,
> With an alien people clutching their gods.
> — T.S. Eliot, *The Journey of the Magi*

Heart

*The old master was never concerned with a lump of flesh
Or with the seat of passion:
He went for the heart of the matter.*

*There he is, pointing to the moon —
Its cool light fills the night sky.*

*One hundred thousand verses!
Do you need more than this?*

One word — Ah!

*If you look at his finger,
More words won't help.*

One hundred thousand verses.
Twenty-five thousand.
Eight thousand.
One page.
A single syllable.

All to describe nothing!

Well, at least they're getting closer.

> Shortly after her husband of many years passed away, an elderly woman came to see a young doctor.
>
> "What's wrong?" he asked.
>
> "My heart is broken."
>
> The doctor listened to her heart with his stethoscope and ran a couple of tests.
>
> When he had finished, he turned to her and said, "I can't find anything wrong with your heart."

People cling to words, and you can't do a thing about it.

Notes

One hundred thousand verses ... to describe nothing!
Several sutras focus on the perfection of wisdom. The longest is *The Perfection of Wisdom in 100,000 Verses*, the shortest is the single syllable "Ah". (As the source of all speech, "Ah" is used as a symbol for emptiness and the perfection of wisdom.) In between are *The Perfection of Wisdom in 25,000 Lines*, *The Perfection of Wisdom in 8,000 Lines*, *The Heart of the Perfection of Wisdom*, etc. Other sutras of this genre are *The Lankavatara Sutra*, *The Vimalakirtinirdesha Sutra*, and *The Diamond Sutra*.

If you look at his finger
When you ask a friend to show you where something is and he points, it makes no sense to look at his or her finger. You have to look to where the finger points. In the same way, when a teacher points to the emptiness of all experience using words or symbols, the meaning is lost if the student tries to understand them instead of looking at what they are pointing to.

My heart is broken
This story comes from James Hillman (1926 -   )

Lady

*You look and look
Yet never see her.*

*She whispers a spell:
The mirror clears
And is not there.*

*She sees you for a moment and...
There!
You know what you are.*

Where is she — right now?

Ordinarily, you are under a spell: two, not one. But when you look into your lover's eyes, you fall into another enchantment: one, not two.

This lady breaks all spells — not one, not two, nothing whatsoever.

Look at a thought, a feeling, or a sensation. Then look at what is aware. What are you looking at?

If you don't know how to jump off a bottomless cliff, ask that scoundrel over there — yes, the one pounding rice.

Notes

Lady
Sanskrit: *bhagavati* (Tib. bcom 'das ldan ma). The term has the sense of both destruction (overcoming the distortions of emotional reaction and conceptual knowing, the four demonic obsessions, etc.) and fortune (the six manifestations of the five aspects of pristine awareness). See *The Heart Sutra Explained*, Donald Lopez, pg. 24 ff. The masculine form (*bhagavan*) is often translated *Lord*. As the term has an implicit sense of nobility, the English feminine form, *Lady*, seems suitable.

Yet never see her
> It doesn't exist: even buddhas do not see it.
> It doesn't not exist: it is the basis of samsara and nirvana.
> — Rangjung Dorje (Karmapa III), *Aspirations for Mahamudra*

She whispers a spell
The original meaning of the word *mantra* was *spell*. The spell here is the Perfection of Wisdom.

the one pounding rice
Hui-neng, the sixth patriarch in the Ch'an (Zen) tradition, was working as a rice-pounder in the monastery's kitchen when he submitted the following poem as an expression of his understanding:
> *Bodhi really has no tree*
> *Nor the clear mirror a stand*
> *Nothing is there initially.*
> *Where do the dust motes land?*
>   (adapted from a translation by Derek Lin)

Perfection

He came this far,
But now the waters of life
Stand in his way.

One by one
He lets them go,
Thought, emotion, identity, and belief.

Without boat or raft or crystal canoe,
He arrives
On the other shore.

Because he is blind, he isn't confused by what others see.
Because he doesn't reach for what isn't there, he goes nowhere.
Because he knows how things are, he arrives on the other shore.

Where is the other shore?

For generosity, nothing to own.
For ethics, nothing to hide.
For patience, nothing to fear.
For effort, nothing to achieve.
For stable attention, nothing to wander.
For wisdom, nothing to know.

lets them go
> *Perfection is finally attained not when there is no longer anything to add but when there is no longer anything to take away...*
> — Antoine de Saint-Exupéry (1900 - 1944)

crystal canoe
From an old Celtic fairy tale, *Connla and the Fairy Maiden*.

the other shore
The Sanskrit *paramita* (Tib. pha rol tu phyin pa) is usually rendered as *perfection*. This is not an ideal word, but probably the best available in English. *Paramita* itself carries the idea of "going to the other shore" and points to the quality of action that is not based on a sense of separation between "I" and "other".

For generosity, nothing to own
In Mahayana Buddhism, those aspiring to awaken use the six perfections (paramitas) — generosity, morality, patience, effort, meditative stability, and wisdom — as ways to step out of the dualistic framework of conventional virtue.

Wisdom

Such a heavy word —
No one can carry it.

Everybody has it —
But few know it.

You say you can't talk about it?
You are right.

That's the point.

Can you acquire wisdom? In the same way that you might acquire a house, the admiration of others, beautiful shoes, a promotion, a lover, or fame?

And if you have it, what do you do with it? Show it off to your friends? Or your enemies?

Wisdom comes in many forms.

You may not recognize it when it comes knocking. Naropa should have known this before he took on Tilopa's sister.

When you don't know what to say, stop — stop everything.
Feel your feet on the ground.

Listen to what everyone is saying, outside and inside.

If (or when) you know what to say, how do you know?

No one can carry it
Wisdom (or *wise*) has an associated word game (as Wittgenstein uses the term) similar to the word *promiscuous*: we rarely use the term to describe ourselves.

Naropa should have known this before he took on Tilopa's sister
Naropa was one of the leading scholars and debaters at Nalanda University in the 11th century. One day, he returned to his room to find a horrifically ugly woman rummaging through his texts. When she asked him if he understood the words, he replied, "Yes." She immediately started to dance, laughing and jumping about gleefully. Then she asked if he understood the meaning. Hoping to please her again, he said, "Yes." To his surprise, she collapsed in tears, sobbing and wailing hysterically. When he asked why, she replied, "You told the truth when you said you understood the words, but you didn't tell the truth when you said you understood the meaning. See my brother, Tilopa." She then turned into a whirlwind and disappeared.

The Invocation

> I bow to Lady Perfection of Wisdom

Respect the gods and buddhas, but don't rely on them.
— Miyamoto Musashi (1584 - 1645)

I bow to Lady Perfection of Wisdom

Some worship a golden goddess
With four arms, a book, and a rosary —
Expecting, perhaps, to be freed from pain.

Some worship a collection of sacred tomes
Full of subtle concepts and subtler logic —
Confident, perhaps, in the power of reason.

Some worship bliss, clarity, emptiness,
Or other altered states —
Convinced, perhaps, that there is something to gain.

Apparently no one told them
How to bow.

"Who sings?" asked a jazz singer.

One night she disappeared from the nightclub stage, but the song continued, and the audience loved it.

Apparently she knew how to bow.

Devotion may be a path, but worship just makes things worse. There's nothing outside to free you, and nothing inside either.

Bow, and bow, and bow again.

With each bow, ask, "Who is bowing?"

bliss, clarity, emptiness
As meditation practice matures, three kinds of experience arise: experiences of physical and mental bliss, experiences of clear states of mind (including clairvoyance, etc.), and experiences of non-thought and emptiness. Attachment to these states is an impediment to recognizing and living in natural awareness.

Devotion may be a path, but worship just makes things worse.
The cultivation of powerful experiences of loving kindness, compassion, or devotion raise the level of energy in attention. However, in worship, people tend to idealize the focus of devotion and this idealization reinforces patterns of emotional projection and dualistic perception.

The Setting

Thus have I heard. At one time Lord Buddha was staying at Vulture Peak Mountain in Rajagriha, with a great gathering of the monastic sangha and the bodhisattva sangha.

At that time, Lord Buddha entered an absorption, called *Profound Radiance*, in which all elements of experience are present.

At the same time, noble Avalokiteshvara, the bodhisattva mahasattva, was looking right at the experience of the profound perfection of wisdom and he saw the five groups to be empty of nature.

I was not here until you came;
And I shall not be here when you are gone.
— Edwin Arlington Robinson, *Why He Was There*

Thus have I heard.

*Forty years, and
He had only the words.*

Lucky for us!

*If he had really listened,
He might not have said
Anything.*

Five conditions for teaching to take place:

A time — right now.
A place — right here.
A teacher — hmm, that's a bit trickier. What about your own mind?
A teaching — what you are holding in your hand.
And a student — you, if you are up for it.

You've probably heard everything you need to hear already. But, here you are, reading this book. Why?

Ananda was in the same boat. He heard everything Buddha taught. His wonderful memory faithfully retained all the words, but the meaning? For that, he had to wait until Buddha was dead, in more ways than one.

Words are only a means to an end.

Notes

Ananda

Ananda was Buddha Shakyamuni's cousin. He accompanied the Buddha wherever he went and was present at all of his teachings. After Buddha's death, the other disciples relied on Ananda's perfect memory to determine what the Buddha did or did not say. Despite his close association with Buddha, Ananda did not experience awakening while Buddha was alive.

Words are only a means to an end.
  Where can I find a man who has forgotten words so I can have a word with him?
  — Chuang Tzu (370 - 301 BCE)

At one time...

Past, future, present?
This all takes place before time begins
And after time ends.
Why doesn't he set his alarm while he's dreaming?
Then he can wake up when he falls asleep.

Either this never happened and never will happen, or it's happening right now.

Take your pick.

Do you believe in fairy tales? Once upon a time...

At the end of the story, a fairy tale filled with princesses, dragons, and wonderful castles, the child asked her father, "Did it really happen like that?"

He smiled, "I don't know if it happened exactly like that, but I'm sure, if you think about it, you will see that it's all true."

Either this never happened and never will happen, or it's happening right now. When read not as descriptions of actual meetings but as descriptions of presence, of being awake, these sutras have a timeless power to elicit experience and understanding in the reader.

...Lord Buddha was staying at Vulture Peak Mountain in Rajagriha...

Given what the old man said there,
You wonder what the vultures found to pick over.

They say it's the center of the world.

It must be:
The more you try to get there,
The farther away you go.

The vultures must have gone hungry that day because nothing was taught and nothing was learned.

That's the secret.

Hold onto the idea that you are going to get somewhere and see how far you go!

This is no looking-glass world, with hills so high they make other hills look like valleys, and where you have to walk away from your destination if you want to get there.

Remember, after the old man died, no one wrote about this for several hundred years.

Notes

old man
Buddha Shakyamuni

the center of the world
In ancient Buddhist cosmology, India was regarded as the central country because Buddha lived there. In the Mahayana tradition, Rajagriha (present day Rajgir) was regarded, mythically, as the center of the world because Buddha taught many of the Perfection of Wisdom sutras there.

The farther away you go
In *Through the Looking Glass*, Alice finds that when she walks toward the house, she ends up farther and farther away.

make other hills look like valleys
From Lewis Carroll's *Through the Looking Glass*: "When you say 'hill,' " the Queen interrupted, "I could show you hills, in comparison with which you'd call that a valley."

several hundred years
While sutras have, for centuries, been regarded in Tibet and elsewhere as a faithful account of the Buddha's teachings, modern analytical methods have shown that they were written centuries later and record the evolution of various trains of thought in Indian Buddhism. This research suggests that many of the sutras were essentially commentaries on the Buddha's teachings written by the senior teachers of the day, a practice that has sustained Buddhism's vitality in every generation.

> ...with a great gathering of the monastic sangha
> and the bodhisattva sangha.

The solitary pines stand apart
Braving winter winds and summer droughts
Never looking for companions
Or longing for the warmth of another's touch.

Majestic clouds
Soar in the morning sun,
Towering higher than the mind can reach.
After the rain, a sea of bright red blossoms
Where bees hunt for nectar.

It's easy to get lost in a crowd,
But perhaps not this one:
Everyone has the same aim and
Nobody is going anywhere.

Just walk away from the whole mess. Then desire naturally fades away, no?

Or step into life completely and let it illumine your mind. This takes heart. Maybe you didn't know you had taken on such an awesome responsibility.

If you're not clear about what you're doing, you fall into confusion and the world falls with you.

One intention — to be free — yet everyone has to find their own way.

Do you know where you're going?

Notes

The solitary pines stand apart
The monastic sangha, with *sravakas* (listeners) and *pratyekabuddhas* (independent buddhas), symbolizes a path of renunciation.

Majestic clouds.
The bodhisattva sangha symbolizes a path that embraces life in the union of compassion and emptiness.

the mind can reach
In the sutras, the qualities and attainments of bodhisattvas are so mythologized that, taken literally, they make awakening seem all but impossible for ordinary people.

an awesome responsibility
The bodhisattva vow is the intention to awaken completely in order to help all other beings become free of suffering.

Do you know where you're going?
  Without running away, I stop going into samsara.
  Without going anywhere, I arrive at buddhahood.
    — Kyer-gong-pa (Tib. skyer gong pa chos kyi seng ge),
    Recognizing Your Mind as the Guru

At that time, Lord Buddha entered an absorption, called *Profound Radiance*, in which all elements of experience are present.

Now what's he doing — counting snowflakes?
What is this profound radiance?
The ex-prince knows but isn't telling.

Four problems, and you can't do a thing about them:
So close you can't see it.
So deep you can't fathom it.
So simple you can't believe it.
So good you can't accept it.

The word is
Don't count, don't examine, don't do anything at all.

Scholars confuse things with intimidating terminology and fine distinctions.

Awareness, by itself, is profound and radiant, yet even the buddhas can't tell you about it.

Anything they said would be a lie, as Vimalakirti knew.

Notes

experience
In this context, the word "dharma" is usually translated as "phenomenon", a rendering that reinforces the subject-object framework. Here, I use the term "experience", regarding dharmas as units of experience, consistent with the view of the Sarvastivadins, on which the *Heart Sutra* is based. See Red Pine's *The Heart Sutra*, pg. 15ff.

counting snowflakes
An image from the Dzogchen and Mahamudra traditions: the arising and releasing of thoughts in awareness is compared to snowflakes landing on a hot stone.

The ex-prince
The traditional accounts of Buddha's life portray him as the son of the king of a small realm in northern India who renounced his family, position, and inheritance to pursue the life of a religious mendicant.

Four problems
In the Amulet Mahamudra of the Shangpa tradition, these are known as the four faults of natural awareness.

as Vimalakirti knew
In the *Vimalakirtinirdesha Sutra*, Vimalakirti, a layman, is ill. When Buddha and his disciples visit him, Vimalakirti asks them "What is the door to non-duality?" and refutes their responses one by one. When Buddha asks Vimalakirti for a response to his own question, Vimalakirti says nothing.

At the same time, noble Avalokiteshvara...

He sees everything.
Is that what makes him noble?

But if he'd actually made any progress,
He wouldn't have all those eyes.

And your gravity fails and negativity don't pull you through...
Maybe despair has its uses.

What would you have done?

Progress — the seducer of the modern world, *la belle dame sans merci.*

One look in her wild, wild eyes, and your life is hers.

Remember, freedom's just another word...

Despair is the mother of humility, a humility that leads to the path of the ancients.

That seems to be what happened to a half-naked fakir, a dreamer, and a music lover.

Notes

He sees everything.
Avalokiteshvara is the bodhisattva (awakening being) who embodies the ideal of awake compassion. The name means "one who looks over all the world". In Tibetan, he is known as Chenrezi (spyan ras gzigs). In China, this bodhisattva became androgynous and then female and is now known as Kuan Yin. In Japan, she becomes Kannon.

He wouldn't have all those eyes.
After working to help beings for three incalculably long eons, Avalokiteshvara despaired at the lack of any sign of any tangible progress. He lost his awakened intention and his head burst into a thousand pieces, according to his original vow. As he renewed his intention to help beings, the thousand pieces of his head became a thousand arms, each with an eye in the palm of the hand, symbolizing the union of compassion and wisdom.

And your gravity fails and negativity don't pull you through...
— Bob Dylan, *Just Like Tom Thumb Blues*

her wild, wild eyes
> She took me to her elfin grot,
>   And there she wept, and sigh'd full sore,
> And there I shut her wild wild eyes
>   With kisses four.
> — John Keats, *La Belle Dame Sans Merci*

freedom's just another word...
— Kris Kristofferson, *Ballad of Me and Bobby McGee*

Despair is the mother of humility
> Death is the mother of beauty; hence from her,
> Alone, shall come fulfillment to our dreams
> And our desires.
> — Wallace Stevens, *Sunday Morning*

the path of the ancients
In one form of the bodhisattva vow (the vow to awaken in order to help all beings), one forms the intention to train and follow in the footsteps of previous bodhisattvas.

half-naked fakir, a dreamer, and a music lover
Gandhi, Martin Luther King, and Nelson Mandela respectively. All spent long periods in jail, often in solitary confinement. At Gandhi's meeting with the Viceroy of India, Churchill referred to him as a half-naked fakir. Martin Luther King's "I have a dream" speech is one of the great calls to compassion and action in the modern era. And, for Nelson Mandela, music was a deep love and source of inspiration during his incarceration.

A big heart, for sure,
But how do you measure these things?
Brave, too, they say, but in the face of what?

The last I heard
There was no one to save.

Why all the fuss?

Compassion is just natural awareness expressing itself. Why do you think people, before they die, want to pass on to others what they have learned?

The more present you are, the more you see how things are, and the more clearly you see how to respond. What may seem remarkable or wonderful to others you see as simply what needs to be done.

Awake mind, big mind — such labels are for those who don't see things as they are. You do what needs doing — brushing your teeth, making your bed, saving the world, taking your children to school. In the end, aren't you just taking care of the only world you experience?

No one expects to be patted on the back for that!

How are you going to save the world? And who are you saving, anyway?

Notes

bodhisattva mahasattva
Literally *awakening being, great being,* the phrase is the formal honorific for the higher (eighth to tenth level) bodhisattvas.

There was no one to save.
> *And though I thus liberate countless beings, not a single being is liberated. And why not? Subhuti, a bodhisattva who creates the perception of a being cannot be called a "bodhisattva".*
> — Buddha, *The Diamond Sutra*

the only world you experience
There are two worlds, the world we experience and the world we think we experience. The world we experience consists of awareness of three things, thoughts, feelings, and sensory sensations. The world we think we experience, that is, family, work, even our body, is constructed from these thoughts, feelings, and sensations. We label particular groups of apparently recurring experiences as *spouse, child, car, flower,* etc. We forget that these are only labels and take the projected objects to be real.

to save the world
> *I couldn't trust the thinking of a man who takes the Universe —
> if there is one — for granted... I only decide about my Universe...
> My Universe is my eyes and ears. Anything else is hearsay.*
> — Douglas Adams, *The Restaurant at the End of the Universe*

> ...was looking right at the experience
> of the profound perfection of wisdom...

He watches the wind sweep over grasslands
Until the blue dust of distant fields
Merges with the summer sky,
And doesn't see a thing.

He listens to the intricacies of
Point and counterpoint,
Canon and fugue,
As his niece practices her piano,
But doesn't hear a sound.

His mouth fills with the succulent flavors
Of lichee and mango,
Quince and pomegranate,
But he doesn't taste a thing.

Is he dead?
Perhaps,
But he's more alive than most.

Not with his eyes did he look, nor with any of the other senses. And not with his mind — that was nowhere to be found.

He makes it sound so important, so difficult, so subtle, and so mysterious. Yet he just sits there, looking at nothing.

What's so special about that?

Caught up in what you are going to do,
you don't know what you are doing.

Caught up in what you are going to say,
you don't know what you are saying.

Caught up in what you are going to hear,
you don't know what you are hearing.

Caught up in what you are going to be,
you don't know what you are.

Notes

was looking right at the experience

This phrase is often translated simply as *practice*, a rendering that doesn't bring out the meaning of the main verb in the sentence, which is *to look* (Tib. lta ba). *Experience* in this context refers to engagement in the perfection of wisdom, both the dropping of the subject-object framework and the awareness that is naturally present when the subject-object framework has dropped away.

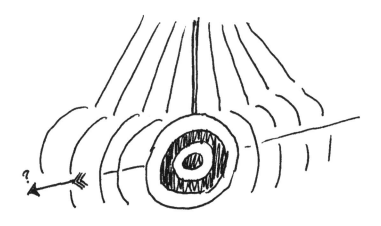

>   ...and he saw the five groups to be empty of nature.

In the end, it's all empty,
But, is it like a room,
Like milk, or yoghurt,
Or like the horns of a rabbit,
Or a secret that cannot be put into words?

What is experience?

It's not an empty room: there's too much going on.

It doesn't come from anywhere and it doesn't go anywhere, so don't eat the yoghurt, and forget the milk.

Have you ever seen the horns of a rabbit?

Experience — what can you say about it?

Nothing whatsoever.

_____ Notes

the five groups
Skt. *skandha* (Tib. phung po). This term is often translated as "aggregate", but the translation is misleading as it conveys the idea of things coming together. The skandhas are simply five groups into which the different elements of experience (dharmas) are categorized: sensory experience (form), emotional tones associated with sensory experience (feeling), names used to refer to experience (concept), emotional reactions to experience (mental formation), and consciousness of experience (consciousness).

like a room, /milk, or yoghurt /the horns of a rabbit /a secret
Five traditional similes for different meanings of emptiness: empty space, producing no result, having no genesis, non-existence, and mystery.

Nothing whatsoever
　Of what one cannot speak, one must be silent.
　　— Ludwig Wittgenstein, *Tractatus Logico-Philosophicus*

The Question

Then, through the power of the Buddha, venerable Shariputra
asked noble Avalokiteshvara, the bodhisattva mahasattva,
"How does a son or daughter of the noble family, who wishes to
practice the profound perfection of wisdom, train?"

You lose your grip, and then you slip
Into the Masterpiece
— Leonard Cohen, *Thousand Kisses Deep*

Then, through the power of the Buddha...

Pushing people around, is he?
What does this have to say
About the last words of an old man?

If you pick strawberries while a rat gnaws at a branch,
You will know all about this power.

Work out your own freedom! Why, then, did he not resist nudging his chief disciple? And why didn't he help Ananda?

The consequence — useless arguments that have raged for centuries.

If awakening comes through the power of another, how can you know it?
If it comes through your own power, how can you not know it?

If all experience is empty, how do you know what to do?
If only samsara is empty, how do you know you are free?

When you hold your hands for meditation,
do you let your thumbs just touch?
When you hold your hands for meditation,
do you let a piece of paper just slip through?

People will argue about anything!

Notes

If you pick strawberries while a rat gnaws at a branch
A traditional Zen koan. You are hanging over a cliff, holding onto a thin branch. Above, a rat is gnawing at the branch. Below, a tiger paces back and forth, waiting for you to fall. In the side of a cliff, you see a strawberry plant with one ripe berry. How does the berry taste?

Work out your own freedom
According to tradition, the Buddha's last words were, "Everything that comes together ends by falling apart. Work out your own freedom."

power of another/own power
A long-standing debate in the Mahayana traditions of Buddhism is "Does awakening come through one's own effort (self-power) or through the compassionate power of buddha, awake mind (other-power)?"

experience is empty/samsara is empty
A long-standing debate in the Tibetan tradition about the ultimate nature of experience takes place around the question "Is all experience empty (self-emptiness) or is experience empty only of the factors that generate samsara (other-emptiness)?"

People will argue about anything
Nyoshul Khenpo (1932-1999) often used the example of thumbs touching or not touching in the traditional way one positions the hands for meditation to illustrate the pointlessness of debate.

> ...venerable Shariputra asked noble Avalokiteshvara,
> the bodhisattva mahasattva...

Who let him in?

Maybe there is life in the old dog.
He's been barking up this tree for years
But has reached the end of his chain.

He didn't dare go to Vimalakirti.

A sharp intellect can only do so much.
To go further,
Sharper eyes are needed —

The eyes of compassion?

Advice from a snake charmer: Don't say a word! As soon as you open your mouth, you contradict yourself.

You have to rely on this logic if you are going to get anywhere.

Take a page from Alice.

You know you're in trouble when you develop a theory of everything.

When the intellect fails, well... There's always the heart.

Notes

Who let him in?
The Sarvastivadins regarded Shariputra as the source of inspiration for their classifications of experience (on which the *Heart Sutra* is based), so who better to be the interlocutor for Avalokiteshvara? Nevertheless, several Indian commentaries undertake lengthy arguments to explain the presence of a follower of the Hinayana at a teaching on the perfection of wisdom, one of the central teachings of the Mahayana.

He didn't dare go to Vimalakirti.
Vimalakirti admonished Shariputra for relying on practice based on behavioral and cognitive restrictions instead of simply being awake and present in the natural flow of human experience. cf.
  Your mind is the source of all experience, patterned or free.
  You awaken completely when you rest and do nothing at all.
  Instead, you follow meticulously and exclusively
  The cycle of teaching on ignorance, interdependence, and samsara.
  — Jigme Lingpa, *The Wisdom Experience of Ever-present Good*

You have to rely on this logic if you are going to get anywhere.
The dialectics of The Middle Way (Skt. *Madhyamaka*) demonstrate that the nature of experience cannot be understood intellectually: experience defies all categorization. One must look for a knowing that is non-conceptual.

Take a page from Alice.
  To be able to see Nobody, and at that distance, too.
  — Lewis Carroll, *Through the Looking Glass*

"How should a son or daughter of the noble family, who wishes
to experience the profound perfection of wisdom, train?"

It didn't seem like much at the time,
A tiny trickle of water
Flowing over brown earth, matted leaves, and grass.

But it carried with it a grain of dirt, then two.

It wasn't long before
The dam
Crumbled.

Impatient waters
Swept away
The manicured vale
As the river returned
To what it always was.

Now he's done it!

Once the question leaves his lips, he can't turn back.

Even if your foot never hits the ground, you have to keep going.

Training, learning? What's he talking about?

Do people actually do this stuff?

They say it comes naturally.

Still, the question had to be asked.

Notes

As the river returned
To what it always was
   And the ragged rock in the restless waters,
   Waves wash over it, fogs conceal it;
   On a halcyon day it is merely a monument,
   In navigable weather it is always a seamark
   To lay a course by: but in the sombre season
   Or the sudden fury, is what it always was.
   —T.S. Eliot, *The Dry Salvages*

The Answer

> Addressed in this way, noble Avalokiteshvara, the bodhisattva mahasattva, said to venerable Shariputra, "O Shariputra, a son or daughter of the noble family who wishes to practice the profound perfection of wisdom looks in this way: see the five groups to be truly empty of nature.

Those who know do not talk.
Those who talk do not know.
— Lao Tzu, *Tao Te Ching*

> Addressed in this way, noble Avalokiteshvara,
> the bodhisattva mahasattva, said to venerable Shariputra…

What is he going to do:

Talk about buddha nature?
Ask where your face was before you were born?
Tell you the first truth?

Inexpressible!
Inconceivable!
Indescribable!

Apparently he's not listening.

A Chinese master lay ill, very ill. A close student came to him, and asked, "Dear master, please tell me the first truth."

The old man smiled and said, "I will."

Days passed, and the master's health continued to wane. Again, the student approached. "Please, master, please tell me the first truth."

"I will," said his teacher, "but this is not the time."

Soon after, the signs that death would soon come were clearly evident. Desperate, the student approached his teacher a third time with the same request.

With his last ounce of strength, the master looked gently at him, gazing with an extraordinary clarity deep into the student's eyes. In a barely audible whisper, he said, "Ah… If I tell you the first truth… it will become… the second."

Then his eyes closed and he died.

Notes

buddha nature
In the Mahayana teachings, buddha nature is present in all beings. What is buddha nature? According to Kongtrul the Great, it's what remains when all the confusion of samsaric experience is cleared away.

where your face was before you were born
This famous koan from the life of Hui-neng, the sixth patriarch, points directly to original knowing.

Inexpressible!
Inconceivable!
Indescribable!
From a verse in praise of the perfection of wisdom:
> *Perfection of Wisdom, inexpressible, inconceivable, indescribable,*
> *Not created, not restricted, just like the sky,*
> *The experience of pristine awareness, knowing itself:*
> *To the mother of the buddhas of the three times, I bow.*
> — Rahulabhadra, *In Praise of the Mother*

"O Shariputra, a son or daughter of the noble family who wishes
to practice the profound perfection of wisdom looks in this way:
see the five groups to be truly empty of nature.

Forget about looking.
That's just how you keep your distance.

To see
You have to
Step into the jaws of experience.

Chew and be chewed,
Until nothing is left.

Student: What do I do when I feel hungry?
Teacher: Feel full.

Typical teacher, describing the result and not the method!

You may start with a method, but you soon hanker after results. The rot is inevitable.

You teach what you know, but, for others, it's just dogma.

You create a ritual to celebrate your joy, but for others, it's just an empty form.

You adopt disciplines to support your practice, but for others, they're just rules.

When you are hungry, eat. When you feel full, stop.

describing the result and not the method
Every training discipline has four components: purpose, method, effects, and result. The purpose is the reason for undertaking the training. The method is what you do in the training. Effects are what you experience while doing the training (both pleasant and unpleasant). The result is the experience of the purpose and it comes about because of the training. Many people experience difficulties in meditation and other disciplines because they confuse these four categories, taking purpose as method, or effects as results, etc.
See *Wake Up to Your Life*, Ken McLeod, pg. 58-60 and 248-253.

... just dogma/... just an empty form /... just rules
These three lines describe three forms of degeneration in spiritual traditions (personal communication from David Steindl-Rast).

Emptiness I

> Form is emptiness; emptiness is form.
> Emptiness is not other than form; form is not other than emptiness.
> In the same way, feeling, concept, mental formation, and
> consciousness are emptiness.

Reality is not protected or defended by laws, proclamations, ukases, cannons and armadas. Reality is that which is sprouting all the time out of death and disintegration.
— Henry Miller (1891 – 1980)

Form is emptiness; emptiness is form.

Filaments of fragrance
Rise from a glowing tip,
Spiral in delicate figures
And break into a mass of ephemeral swirls.
Yet the scent of sandalwood lingers in the air.

A beautiful impostor
Stands stiffly
Promising nothing.

Look into her eyes
And ask her
Where she'd be
If you stopped thinking.

Don't tell the arrow-smith:
He thought even cattle knew better.

What is this, this experience you are having — right now?

The threads of life seem so real: family, friends, house, career, triumphs, defeats, war, peace, love, hate, confusion…

Sensations, thoughts, feelings — vivid, seductive, compelling, distracting… Where are they?

What you think is there may not be there.
And what you think is not there may be there.

When you fill a room with furniture, where does the space go?
When a sound breaks the silence, where does the silence go?
When a thought disturbs the stillness of your mind, where does the stillness go?

Notes

He thought even cattle knew better
Saraha, the arrow-smith, one of the eighty-four mahasiddhas (great masters), regarded belief as the problem:
Those who believe in reality are stupid, like cows.
Those who believe in emptiness are even stupider.

Emptiness is not other than form; form is not other than emptiness.

Sweep these two rat turds under the rug!
Where's the rug?

In the long grass
Four doors stand
Mute, closed.
Four doors, no walls.

If you listen carefully,
You'll hear the floorboards
Disappearing —
One by one.

You can't have waves without water.

First you want two, not one. Then you want one, not two.

Disculpa Señora, pero no tenemos ninguno de estos dos platos hoy diá.

You can't go over this. You can't go under it. You can't go around it. And you can't go through it.

Go ahead and think about it. See how your head feels in the morning!

Thousands of words have been written on these lines and they haven't saved a single soul.

If the idea of doors without walls disturbs you, then, by all means, build the walls. But don't complain later about a lack of freedom.

The ceremony of removing the floor:
    Things aren't what they seem.
    Emptiness is not what it seems.
    Opposition is not what it seems.
    Nothing is not what it seems.

Let the monkey run, if it will.

Notes

these two rat turds
cf. Hakuin's commentary on these lines:
> *A nice hot kettle of stew. He ruins it by dropping a couple of rat turds in.*
> — Hakuin, *Zen Words for the Heart*

The rat turds are form and emptiness.

You'll hear the floorboards
Disappearing
The floorboards are the four ontological possibilities (Tib. mu.bzhi): exists, doesn't exist, exists and doesn't exist, neither exists nor doesn't exist.

Disculpa Señora...
Translation: Our apologies, madam, but neither of these items is on the menu today.

Let the monkey run
The thinking mind, with all its chatter and activity, is often compared to a monkey. In the direct awareness traditions, once the practitioner has experienced the nature of being, he or she is encouraged to do nothing and just let awareness sort itself out.

In the same way, feeling, concept, mental formation, and consciousness are emptiness.

Plop!
The rings
Widen
Across the pond.

Nothing escapes
Their inexorable advance.

Mr. Frog?
He's long gone.

Here they are, lined up for inspection.

You can search every one of them, but you won't find anything.

What are you waiting for?

> *Feeling is emptiness.*
> *Emptiness is feeling.*
> *Emptiness is not other than feeling.*
> *Feeling is not other than emptiness.*

The rest are up to you.

> *To meditate means to be aware of what is going on. What is going on is very important.*
> — Thich Nhat Hanh (1926 -   )

but you won't find anything
This part of the *Heart Sutra* describes one aspect of the mystery of presence: none of the components of experience (i.e., the five groups) exists as a concrete entity in its own right.

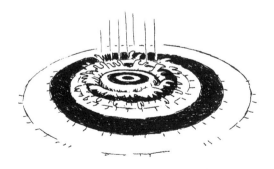

Emptiness II

> Therefore, Shariputra, all experience is emptiness.
> It is not defined. It is not born or destroyed, impure or
> free from impurity, not incomplete or complete.

When the shoe fits, the foot is forgotten.
— Chuang Tzu (370 - 301 BCE)

Therefore, Shariputra, all experience is emptiness. It is not defined.

You follow the trail
Up steep mountain passes
Over arid deserts
Through swamps, forests, meadows, cities, and caves
Looking for
That one reference point
To tell you
Where you are
Once and for all.

You think you can define things, say what they really are? Okay, what is "big"? Depends on how big you are, doesn't it? To mathematicians, a doughnut and a cup are the same, but don't try dunking a cup into your coffee.

Experience arises. It isn't a thing. You can't trade it, share it, or give it away. And no one can dispute it.

This may be a blessing, a curse, or a path.

Teach people to doubt their experience and you take away their lives. Teach people not to doubt their experience and you make them into monsters.

In the end, things are neither true nor not true.

How do you live with that?

Notes

It is not defined.
(Tib. mtshan nyid med pa) This term means *no defining attributes or characteristics*. No experience can be reduced to a set of intrinsic characteristics. All experiences are, in the end, combinations of interdependent thoughts, feelings, and sensations. There is no "thing" to which to apply a label.

a doughnut and a cup are the same
Both objects have the common property of having one hole — the loop of the cup handle in one case, the hole in the doughnut, the other. In order to define such properties mathematically, all other properties have to be ignored.

You can't trade it, share it, or give it away
> *We have become so accustomed to the world of giving and taking that we assume it is only normal to trade with another, and we lose sight of that life wherein trading has no bearing.*
> — Uchiyama Roshi, *How to Cook Your Life*

It is not born or destroyed...

Another couple of impostors
In brilliant disguise.
They've fooled almost everyone:
Just look at the world.

Things change.
Things aren't what they seem.
Where is here?
When is now?

Don't be distracted.
Such questions aren't for the faint-hearted.

Many years ago in Sarnath, a young Western student of Buddhism asked a Tibetan teacher, "Where are time and space in the five groups?" A reasonable question, perhaps. But the response was: "For whom?"

> A man learns that, on such and such a day, all the water in the world will change and anyone who drinks it will go crazy. He saves water in a large cistern and waits. On the fated day, the water changes. One by one, people drink it and they go crazy. The man continues to drink the old water. There comes a day, however, when he abandons his cistern, drinks the new water, and goes crazy, too. But to everyone else, it seems that he has recovered from insanity.

The ancients saw things differently:
> Where do things come from before we experience them?
> Where are they while we experience them?
> Where do they go after we experience them?

They thought people who could answer these questions were crazy. Most people, today, would say the ancients were crazy.

Notes

Another couple of impostors
The impostors are space and time. When a sense of self is operating, they are experienced as external absolutes in which perception and thought are ordered. Einstein showed that the view of time and space as externals places limits on perception. Buddhism sees time and space as frameworks created by a sense of self that stands apart from experience.

brilliant disguise
> *So tell me what I see when I look in your eyes*
> *Is that you baby or just a brilliant disguise*
> —Bruce Springsteen, *Brilliant Disguise*

all the water in the world will change
Another telling of this story is found in *Tales of the Dervishes*, Idries Shah

...not impure or free from impurity...

To hear
The most beautiful song
In the world
You have to be lashed to a mast.

Only when
You've finished
Raking
Will you learn about true perfection.

Life's tough.
Even buddhas have to wash their faces.

Enough!
Just let things be.

How many wars does purity cause? Pure food, pure body, pure art, pure life, pure morals, pure ideology, pure practice, pure mind…
The list goes on and on.

Is this being awake, or merely trying to avoid discomfort?

What is dirt?

The difference is in your mind.

And what about your mind is impure? …or pure?

One fall day, a monk carefully raked up all the leaves that had fallen on the lawn in front of the monastery. At the end of the day, the abbot came to look at his work.

"Isn't it perfect?" asked the monk, pointing proudly at the immaculate lawn.

"Not quite," said the abbot. He walked over to a tree in the middle of the lawn and shook it vigorously. It brushed against other trees, and leaves from all of them floated down to the ground. "Now it is," he smiled.

Notes

The most beautiful song
In the world
The song of the Sirens was so pure and so beautiful that it made men jump off their ships and swim to their death. In order to hear the Sirens' song and avoid the fate of others, Odysseus plugged the ears of his men with wax and had them tie him to the mast of his ship.

Even buddhas have to wash their faces
  No one gets dirty living in the world of men.
  Not a clean face in all the Buddhas' pure lands.
    — Hakuin, Zen Words for the Heart.

...and not incomplete or complete.

*A long ride out,
And he enjoyed every minute of it.*

*The return took only a moment.
But what happened to his wife
And his children
Remained
A mystery
Forever.*

*Don't take it personally:
There was nothing here before you came
And there won't be anything here after you go.*

He keeps laying it on, one insult after another.

At the first gate, you drop ideas; at the second, dreams. Now you've arrived at the third. What are you going to leave here?

"The experience was incomplete," you say.

Nonsense. That's just your way of saying you weren't satisfied.

No ground, no base. What's missing?

*The thief left it behind —
the moon
At the window.*
— Ryokan, One Robe, One Bowl

Notes

A mystery
Forever
See the story *The Prince and the Horse*
pg. 2ff, *Wake Up to Your Life*, Ken McLeod

one insult after another
A description of meditation practice attributed to Chogyam Trungpa (1939 - 1987)

At the first gate
This section of the sutra uses the three gates to freedom to negate the three marks of existence: impermanence, suffering, and non-self. The first gate is *no defining characteristics* (not born or destroyed), the second is *no aspiration* (not impure or free from impurity), the third is *emptiness* (not incomplete or complete).

Emptiness III

Therefore, Shariputra, in emptiness, there is no form, no feeling, no concept, no mental formation, no consciousness; no eye, no ear, no nose, no tongue, no body, no mind, no appearance, no sound, no smell, no taste, no touch, no mind object; no eye element up to no mind element and no mind consciousness element; no ignorance, no end of ignorance up to no old age and death, no end of old age and death; no suffering, no origin, no cessation, no path; no pristine awareness, no attainment, and no non-attainment.

When the bird and the book disagree, always believe the bird.
— John Audubon (1785 - 1851)

Therefore, Shariputra, in emptiness...

She breathes the same air.
She treads the same ground.
She wears the same clothes.
She eats the same food.

She isn't out there.
She isn't in here.

You don't know where she is!

Can you trust this not knowing?

I'd like to see either of them climb in or out of emptiness! He can get away with this nonsense only because everyone's asleep.

People took him at his word and started to talk about emptiness — big emptiness, little emptiness, inner emptiness, outer emptiness. Sixteen in all, or was it twenty?

A hunter and his pals didn't know whether to laugh or cry, but they did know how to find her.

Notes

Sixteen in all, or was it twenty
One list of the sixteen kinds of emptiness: the emptiness of sense objects, the emptiness of sense faculties, the emptiness of sensing, the emptiness of emptiness itself, the emptiness of what is great, the emptiness of what is ultimate, the emptiness of conditioned experience, the emptiness of unconditioned experience, the emptiness of what is not a position, the emptiness of what has no beginning or end, the emptiness of what is not given up, the emptiness of essence, the emptiness of all experience, the emptiness of defining attributes, the emptiness of what doesn't exist, the emptiness of things consisting of non-things. See *Meditations on Emptiness*, Jeffrey Hopkins.

A hunter and his pals
Savaripa, one of the eighty-four great masters of medieval Indian Buddhism. They relied on the direct experience of emptiness, not on classifications or other academic schemes.

> ...there is no form, no feeling, no concept,
> no mental formation, no consciousness...

He's been fishing in these buckets
For thousands of years
And never had a nibble.

He continues to study them,
Seeking to unlock the mystery of fish.

Useless pails, full of holes —
Throw them away!

What am I?

Not form. It seems solid, but it always has parts.

Not feeling. Too fleeting, and which one, anyway?

Not concept. I have too many names already.

Not mental formation. Too fluid — sometimes I'm sad, sometimes I'm glad, sometimes I'm mad, and sometimes I'm bad.

Not consciousness. I may be conscious but not consciousness.

He'd have better luck looking for a chariot in his dreams.

Notes

no form, no feeling, no concept, no mental formation, no consciousness
The five-group (five skandha) map of experience classifies the components of ordinary experience into five groups: form, feeling, concept, mental formation, and consciousness. The purpose of this map is to eliminate the notion of a permanent, independent self by showing that no such entity is present in any of the five groups.

Seeking to unlock the mystery of fish
A study of the skandhas as entities doesn't help you know the mystery of your own being.

a chariot
A classical analogy for this analysis is to determine where the essence of "chariot" resides: in the wheels, in the axle, in the carriage, etc.

...no eye, no ear, no nose, no tongue, no body, no mind, no form, no sound, no smell, no taste, no touch, no mind object...

When I looked into her eyes,
There were only the eyes.

When our lips met,
There was only the kiss.

When I awoke, she was not there.

The dream's fragrance gently lingered.

Go play on half a teeter-totter. How much fun is that?

With his demons Milarepa kept his distance. Much good that did him.

Don't push it away. It's not something other.

Hang from a cliff or go to a concert. Eyes, ears, nose — they all disappear.

The world is given to me only once, not one existing and one perceived. Subject and object are only one. The barrier between them cannot be said to have broken down as a result of recent experience in the physical sciences, for this barrier does not exist.
    — Erwin Schrödinger (1887 - 1961)

no eye, no ear, no nose, no tongue, no body, no mind, no form, no sound, no smell, no taste, no touch, no mind object
The twelve-field map classifies experience into content (one for each of the six sensory objects) and experience of content (one for each of the six sensing abilities with the corresponding faculty and consciousness combined). The purpose of this map is to eliminate the notion of a self as a perceiving subject by showing that no perception takes place without both subject and object.

Go play on half a teeter-totter
Pointing out the futility of regarding subject and object as separate entities.

Milarepa kept his distance
When Milarepa, the great Tibetan poet-hermit, encountered five demons in his cave, he tried various means to get rid of them. As long as he regarded them as external objects, he was helpless. See *The Tale of Red Rock Jewel Valley*, in *The Hundred Thousand Songs of Milarepa*.

> ...no eye element up to no mind element and
> no mind consciousness element...

Here they come,
The three musketeers.
One of them has to be responsible for this mess.
"One for all, and all for one!"

The inquisitor, with no one left to question,
Slinks away,
A ghost
Forever chasing shadows.

"Eye, do you see?"

"Only when there is shape or color."

"Shape and color, are you responsible for sight?

"When does a falling tree make a sound?"

"Then, sight consciousness, you're the key!"

"What can I do without eye or shape?"

Eight elephants spent several centuries discussing the matter. Vast tomes now collect dust on library shelves. The books, too, are dust, the dust the elephants left behind.

How fragrant is the idea of a rose?

Notes

no eye element up to no mind element and no mind consciousness element
The eighteen-element map classifies experience into three categories: the sense object, the sense faculty, and the sense consciousness. The purpose of this map is to eliminate the notion of a self as the genesis of experience.

When does a falling tree make a sound
This famous conundrum was inspired by George Berkeley's view that things continue to exist when not perceived by any human being because their ideal forms are always present in God's knowing.

Eight elephants
The eight great Indian philosopher-masters whose works on ontology and epistemology form the classical canon of Mahayana logic and philosophy.

the dust the elephants left behind
>   *The men of old*
>   *Took all they really knew*
>   *With them to the grave.*
>   *And so, Lord, what you are reading there*
>   *Is only the dirt they left behind them.*
>   — Duke Hwan and the Wheelwright,
>   from *The Way of Chuang Tzu*, Thomas Merton

...no ignorance, no end of ignorance up to no old age and death,
no end of old age and death...

The creek tumbles apart
On rotting boards.
The mill wheel turns
This way and that.
Nobody comes here any more.
The miller left
When the axle broke
And mice have eaten all the grain.

Who created this nightmare? Who is the writer, the director, or the producer? Who are the actors? Oh, that's right — Who's on first.

You can't stop it because you don't know where it starts. You can't start it because you don't know where it stops.

To explain all this, they built a big machine: twelve paddles to keep things moving, six rooms to store the grain, stairs up and down. It's kept moving by a snake, a rooster, and a pig chasing each other on a treadmill. Meanwhile, one scary monster eats the whole thing every night.

Shadows vanish in the morning light. No snake, and no rope, either.

_____ Notes

no ignorance, no end of ignorance up to no old age and death, no end of old age and death
The twelve links (Skt. *nidana*) of interdependent origination (Skt. *pratitya samutpada*) comprise another classification of experience used by the Sarvastivadins. The purpose of this map is to show that there is no self as agent, and hence, there is no agent that creates suffering.

Who's on first.
A comedy routine made famous by Abbott and Costello.

twelve paddles to keep things moving
The twelve links of interdependent origination: ignorance, mental formation, name and form, the six sense fields, contact, feeling, attraction, grasping, existence, birth, and aging and death. Experience arises as interactions among these links.

six rooms to store the grain
The six realms: hell being, hungry ghost, animal, human, titan, and god. The realms represent the worlds projected by emotional reactions (anger, greed, instinct, desire, jealousy, and pride respectively).

stairs up and down
Traditional depictions of these elements usually show a path up, leading to happier states, and a path down, to unhappier states.

a snake, a rooster, and a pig
The three poisons: aversion, attraction, and indifference, respectively.

one scary monster
To show that the contents of ordinary experience are subject to impermanence, the wheel of existence, consisting of the twelve links along with the six realms, the paths up and down, and the three poisons, is depicted as being eaten by the Lord of Death.

No snake, and no rope
The six realms of experience are the projections of reactive emotions. When direct knowing is uncovered, projections vanish. A classical example of a reactive emotion is the fear that arises when you mistake a piece of rope for a snake. Once you see that the rope is a rope, the fear disappears. From the perspective of the perfection of wisdom, the rope is also a projection. It doesn't exist as an entity in its own right, either.

...no suffering, no origin, no cessation, no path...

*Gems
Among deer droppings.
The moment you touch them
They vanish.*

*A master healer?
The great physician?
What nonsense!*

*He sees no illness,
Makes no diagnosis,
Knows no cure, and
Prescribes no treatment.*

Take suffering, for instance. You certainly experience it — when you drop a hammer on your foot, or your son tells you that he has a terminal illness, or everything is just perfect in your life but you're not quite there. It's always the same old problem; you want things to be just a little different — a lot.

Stop wanting, they say, and follow this path, right this, right that. Right, wrong, right, left... Such dualisms only go so far. This can't be the path!

In clear open awareness, where is the suffering?

In groundless being, where do things come from?

Where there is no beginning or end, what is there to cease?

When everything is just there, where is the path?

If you try to think this out, you'll be caught in a blizzard. Even a hot stone won't help you then.

Notes

no suffering, no origin, no cessation, no path
In the Sarvastivadin system, the Four Noble Truths map shows that there is no self that is the basis of reaction or response.

Among deer droppings
Buddha Shakyamuni first taught the Four Truths in the Deer Park in Sarnath, outside modern day Varanasi.

A master healer?
The great physician?
Traditional epithets for the Buddha.

He sees no illness
The Four Noble Truths are based on an old Vedic medical model: illness, cause, cure, and treatment.

Even a hot stone
In the second stage of mahamudra practice, simplicity, thoughts release themselves like snowflakes landing on a hot stone.

...no pristine awareness, no attainment, and no non-attainment.

*One can't dip his toe into a river.
Another can't outrun a tortoise.
An old farmer with a long scythe
Stops them both in their tracks.*

*Watch for this swindler.
In his game of give and take,
You'll be left with exactly what you started with.*

What!? No pristine awareness? Give me my money back.

Il faut payer, mais, peut-être tu n'obtiens rien.

I thought this was what the whole trip was about, and here you're saying there's nothing at the end of the road. In fact, you just said there was no road, so I guess you'd say there can't be an end to the road, or an end, or...

Look, we've gone through the whole thing now — no self that exists as an entity, as an experiencer, as the genesis of experience, as an agent, as a controller, as the dominant factor in experience, as the basis of reaction and response, blah, blah, blah. And I'm fine with that. I mean, after all, who needs a self? It's just another thing to lug around.

But I want to be free. I, me, free — hey, you with the thousand eyes, I'm talking to you!

Pristine awareness, that's the ticket, right? Like, isn't that what all the dzogchen boys are endlessly raving about — awareness, realm of totality, suchness, presence, time out of time? You know what I mean.

Now you say that there is no ticket, and I've got nowhere to go, and even if I got somewhere, I wouldn't have gotten anywhere, because there isn't anywhere to get, and if I think there isn't anywhere to get, then I'm not there either.

Next thing you'll be saying is that I'm not where I am and I am where I'm not!
You're worse than a Cheshire cat
and a caterpillar rolled into one.
They just killed size and space.
You're killing time, too!
No, I don't want any jam.

Notes

no pristine awareness, no attainment, and no non-attainment
This final map counteracts any sense of existence through time.

One can't dip his toe into a river.
Heraclitus: "You can't step into the same river twice." This paradox, which poetically summarizes Heraclitus' view of universal change, arises when time is regarded as an entity in its own right.

Another can't outrun a tortoise.
Zeno's paradox about Achilles and the tortoise arises when time is regarded as being finite. Achilles, the most powerful warrior of ancient Greece, is challenged to race against a tortoise. The tortoise has a ten-meter head start. In the time Achilles takes to run the ten meters, the tortoise advances one meter. In the time Achilles takes to run that meter, the tortoise advances another tenth of a meter. Following this logic, Achilles never catches up to the tortoise.

An old farmer with a long scythe
Time: these paradoxes arise only when time is conceived as something separate from experience.

Il faut payer, mais...
Translation: You have to pay, but you may not get anything.

you with the thousand eyes
One of the forms of Avalokiteshvara vividly expresses the union of compassion and wisdom as a thousand hands (compassion) with an eye (wisdom) in the palm of each hand.

Cheshire cat
In Lewis Carroll's *Alice's Adventures In Wonderland*, Alice and the Cheshire cat have the following exchange:
"Would you tell me, please, which way I ought to go from here?"
"That depends a good deal on where you want to get to," said the Cat.
"I don't much care where — " said Alice.
"Then it doesn't matter which way you go," said the Cat.

a caterpillar
Another exchange, between Alice and the Caterpillar:
"I can't explain MYSELF, I'm afraid, sir," said Alice, "because I'm not myself, you see."
"I don't see," said the Caterpillar.

I don't want any jam
The White Queen, to Alice, from Lewis Carroll's *Through the Looking Glass*: "The rule is jam tomorrow and jam yesterday but never jam today."

Emptiness IV

Therefore, Shariputra, because, for bodhisattvas, there is
no attainment, they rest, trusting the perfection of wisdom.
With nothing clouding their minds, they have no fear.
They leave delusion behind and come to the end of nirvana.

Penetrating so many secrets, we cease to believe in the unknowable.
But there it sits nevertheless, calmly licking its chops.
— H. L. Mencken (1880 - 1956)

> Therefore, Shariputra, because,
> for bodhisattvas, there is no attainment...

Not this, not that...
Dewdrops glistening on silver strands —
A jeweled web.
Dewdrops keep falling.
How will you cut through them?

Don't try to follow the reasoning. Maybe it does make sense when you work it all out, but that understanding won't buy you a glass bead in a diamond mine.

Is your machete ready? Good.

Stop striving
to survive, to get your emotional needs met, or to be somebody.

Stop striving
to see things the right way, have the right intention, speak the right way, do the right thing, live the right life, make the right effort, understand things the right way, or focus on the right things.

Stop striving
to intend, sacrifice, or die.

Stop striving
to be generous, moral, imperturbable, productive, undistracted, or intelligent.

Stop striving
to be present, open, or just be.

Stop striving
to stop.

Notes

to survive, to get your emotional needs met, or to be somebody
An alternative wording for the three marks of existence: impermanence, suffering, and non-self.

see things the right way, have the right intention, speak the right way, do the right thing, live the right life, make the right effort, understand things the right way, or focus on the right things
The noble eightfold path, the way of life that Buddha taught. In this context, "right" does not mean right versus wrong, but engaging each of these efforts in attention. See *Wake Up to Your Life*, pg. 28ff.

intend, sacrifice, or die
An alternative wording for the three gates to freedom: no characteristics, no aspiration, and emptiness.

be generous, moral, imperturbable, productive, undistracted, intelligent
The six perfections, the central practice in the Mahayana.

be present, be open, or just be
An alternative wording of the three instructions for mahamudra: don't wander, don't control, don't work at anything (Tib. ma yengs ma bcos ma bsgom).

...they rest, trusting the perfection of wisdom.

In a world of constant movement,
You can't hold anything.
Nor can you hold nothing.
Give up all efforts to make things other than they are.

Listen to the whispers of ten thousand voices.
When no one is left, your way will be clear.

If you trust, in what do you trust?

If you are devoted, what happens to your own knowing?

If you have faith, can you open to whatever your life presents?

If you believe, how do you meet other views?

If you are confident, how do you view other approaches?

If you depend, how do you stand on your own feet?

If you rely, on what do you rely?

As for resting, what breathtaking pretension! He, better than anyone, knows that the work is just beginning.

Notes

trusting
The Tibetan *rten* (pron. ten) is usually rendered *rely on* or *depend on*. I use *trust* because it is closer to my experience. Among my colleagues, opinions on the best English word seem to be divided between rely and trust, depending on the role of devotion in their practice.

the work is just beginning
> Even when full buddhahood is attained, there is nothing to do except work for the welfare of others with non-referential compassion.
> — Jamgön Kongtrul, *The Great Path of Awakening,*
>   translated by Ken McLeod

With nothing clouding their minds, they have no fear.

Oh, how they cloud and confuse you
With their thunderous threats,
Their treacherous lies,
Their blind urges,
Their alluring temptations,
Their jealous resentments,
Their righteous positions,
All deftly calculated to avoid
The mind-numbing, heart-stopping, body-freezing fear
That senses

You are not what you think you are.

It's true.

Ghosts lurk in the darker recesses of your mind, "Just don't forget who you are and how important you are. We are all depending on you. You control everything. You do know that, don't you?"

It's the old business of the two students watching a flag. What do you say?

Clear empty space? No such beast.

If you don't break your ropes while you're alive,
do you think ghosts will do it after?
— Kabir (1440 - 1518)

Notes

clouding their minds
The two fundamental forms of clouding or distortion are emotional reactions and conceptual knowing. Conceptual knowing includes not knowing what one is and conceptual thinking based on dualistic perception. Clouding from emotional reactions includes the emotional reactions themselves and the conditioning (karma) they induce.

two students watching a flag
Two students, watching a flag flapping in the wind, were discussing whether it was the flag that moves or the wind that moves. Hui-neng, the sixth Ch'an (Zen) patriarch, overhearing the discussion, said it is the mind that moves. Later, Wu-men Hui-k'ai (Mumon) said they were all wrong.

They leave delusion behind...

If you seek a home,
  Remember,
She has none.

If you seek comfort,
  Remember,
She opens to everything.

If you seek security,
  Remember,
She cannot be controlled.

If you seek transcendence,
  Remember,
She accepts things just as they are.

You see it in the desperation with which people avoid the topic of death.
You see it again in myths and fairy tales: eternal life, the land of the ever-living.
Will you, too, believe the propaganda when you discover what is undying and changeless?

You see it in the desperation with which people seek happiness, pleasure, fulfillment, or orgasm.
You see it again in myths and fairy tales: eternal happiness, the realm of bliss.
Will you, too, believe the propaganda when you discover freedom from suffering?

You see it in the desperation with which people amass money, power, and position.
You see it again in myths and fairy tales: universal monarch, omniscient lord.
Will you, too, believe the propaganda when you discover that you are everything you experience?

You see it in the desperation with which people seek purity — in food, morality, or traditions.
You see it again in myths and fairy tales: the stainless one, the realm of complete purity.
Will you, too, believe the propaganda when you discover that nothing can compromise you?

Remember, the aim of propaganda is to delude, so that others can use you.

Notes

leave delusion behind
In general, delusion (or error) means to take as real what is not real and to take as unreal what is real. Leaving delusion behind is synonymous with overcoming the four demonic obsessions (the four *maras*): obsession with mortality, obsession with physical existence, obsession with power and control, and obsession with emotional reactions.

...they come to the end of nirvana.

*When did nirvana become
A place to go,
A state to attain?*

People will hide anywhere.

See! He's leaving no stone unturned.

*Maybe it's just knowing
There is nowhere to go
And nothing to do.*

*But you have to take away the hiding places,
All of them.*

It's a bloody business. If you meet the Buddha, you have to kill him. Others go further: first kill the Buddha, then your parents, then your teacher. What's left?

An old eagle from a strange land struggled through Indian jungles, lugging a bag of gold. He watched, helpless, while she threw it away.

A former gatekeeper did everything he could, jumping off a cliff, attacking a princess, even becoming a human bridge. His teacher still had to slap him with his shoe.

With some people you just have to take extreme measures.

Notes

If you meet the Buddha
From the Zen (Ch'an) tradition:
> *If you meet the Buddha on the road, kill him.*
> — Lin Chi (? - 867)

Similar instructions for the student to eliminate any notion of an external referent are found in the Hevajra Tantra and other tantric texts.

first kill the Buddha, then your parents, then your teacher
Instructions in the same vein from the Korean teacher Seung Sahn (1927 - 2004)

An old eagle from a strange land
Khyungpo Naljor (984 - 1139) first journeyed to India at the age of 57 after years of study and practice in Tibet. He sought out Niguma, an Indian adept. To point out the nature of mind, she threw all the gold he offered to her into the jungle, turning the whole world into gold. See *Like an Illusion: Lives of the Shangpa Kagyu Masters,* translated by Nicole Riggs, for a full account of this story.

A former gatekeeper
Naropa (1016 - 1100), left his position as a gatekeeper (a title for leading scholars) at Nalanda University to study under Tilopa. At one point, Tilopa indicated that Naropa should stretch himself across a stream so that Tilopa could walk across without getting wet. While crossing, Tilopa jumped up and down on Naropa's back until Naropa's hands slipped and Tilopa's shoe got wet. Tilopa scolded Naropa, took off his shoe, and slapped Naropa in the face. At that moment, Naropa woke up to the nature of being. See *The Life and Teaching of Naropa*, Herbert Guenther and *Illusion's Game: The Life and Teaching of Naropa*, Chogyam Trungpa.

Awakening

All the buddhas of the three times, by trusting this perfection of wisdom, fully awaken in unsurpassable, true, complete awakening.

When you look into the abyss, the abyss looks into you.
— Friedrich Nietzsche (1844 - 1900)

> All the buddhas of the three times,
> by trusting this perfection of wisdom,...

At the edge of the universe,
At the limit of the world you know,
A leap, perhaps, or is it only a step?

Stand where there is no place to stand.
Rest where there is no place to rest.

Don't pay any attention to that bit about buddhas trusting the perfection of wisdom. He's just stumbling around, crashing into the furniture, hung over from too much meditation.

You're too late. You'll never find a buddha in time.

The buddhas of the past aren't in the past.

The buddhas of the future aren't in the future.

The buddhas of the present aren't in the present.

Where are they?

Notes

the three times
The past, present, and future

You're too late.
Any notion of time takes you out of presence.

...fully awaken in unsurpassable, true, complete awakening.

*The young boy looked at the emperor
And cried out, "Is he insane?"
It's one thing to see things as they are.
It's another to start a campaign.*

With all these fancy, high-sounding words you'd think something special had happened. Or is this a case of "my buddhahood is better than your buddhahood"?

Does awakening stop you from dying?
You can still be shot, poisoned, and, if not, you then have to face the inevitable outcome of old age.

Does it make you more intelligent?
You don't suddenly understand molecular biology, micro-economics, or systems theory.

Does it stop you from being harmed?
You aren't immune to cancer, strokes, or flu bugs.

Does it help you save the world?
Good question. The world may pay attention to you or what you have to say — or not.

It's unsurpassable because there is nowhere to go.
It's true because there is nowhere to hide mistake or error.
It's complete because it includes everything you experience.

Notes

The young boy looked at the emperor
— Hans Christian Anderson, *The Emperor's New Clothes*

my buddhahood is better than your buddhahood
In the end, we are only comparing our experience with ideas and speculation about what others might be experiencing. We can't really compare our experience of eating a strawberry with someone else's, much less know how others experience awakening. We can only know what awakening is and means for us.

The Mantra

> Therefore, the mantra of the perfection of wisdom,
> the mantra of great awareness, the unsurpassed mantra,
> the mantra equal to the unequalled,
> the mantra that completely calms all suffering
> is not a ruse: know it to be true.
>
> Thus, the mantra of the perfection of wisdom is said in this way:
>
> *om gaté gaté paragaté parasamgaté bodhi svaha*
>
> Thus, Shariputra, do all bodhisattva mahasattvas train in the profound perfection of wisdom."

I like talking to Rabbit. He talks about sensible things. He doesn't use long, difficult words like Owl does. He uses short, easy words like 'What about lunch?' and 'Help yourself, Pooh.'
— A. A. Milne, *The House at Pooh Corner*

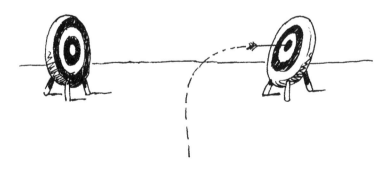

Therefore, the mantra of the perfection of wisdom...

It's a dangerous business,
Breaking enchantments.

When you wake up
From the dream you've been living in,
There's no telling what you will do,
No telling at all.

Mind you,
There's no telling what you will do
In your next dream,
Either.

It's meant to protect you, but this is no ordinary spell.

One aim: natural knowing free from the projections of thought and emotion.

Many people don't know what to make of this possibility. They don't recognize it. They can't stay with it. And they fear its implications.

The best defense is a good offense, they say. It follows that the best defense is total annihilation of the opposition.

Strange. This spell doesn't destroy the opposition; the only thing it destroys is opposition.

How do you engage conflict without opposition?

A king ordered a large boulder to be placed at the center of a major intersection. Entreaties from the rich and the poor fell on deaf ears. He refused to have it moved.

Was this to prove the power of authority or to demonstrate the limitations of an inflexible ruler?

Notes

mantra

A mantra was originally a spell, a magical formula through which a sorcerer could transform people's experience, causing them to see or hear things that weren't there. In Buddhist practice, mantras are used in many ways but all include some element of transforming how one experiences the world and oneself. One folk-etymology for the word defines it as mind (*manas*) protection (*tra*), protecting the mind of the practitioner from distraction, dullness, and emotional confusion.

A king ordered a large boulder...
This story may be found in *Tales of the Dervishes*, Idries Shah.

...the mantra of great awareness,...

There he is, tape in hand,
Measuring the sky.
Next he'll be weighing the wind,
Or calculating the distance between two thoughts.

Take this awareness and give it to someone else.

You can't?

You do have awareness, don't you?

You are not a stone or a lifeless machine.

Good.

Then, give it to a friend just the way you would give him a flower or a book.

You can't, you say.

How do you know you can't?

Now, that's moving in the direction of great awareness!

Notes

calculating the distance between two thoughts
This and the two preceding measurements make as much sense as applying the adjective "great" to awareness. Great in comparison to what?

He's still comparing!
It's a sign:
He isn't quite there.

The old king did this, too,
With his three daughters.

One wouldn't play
And was left with nothing.

Not bad — for a princess.

The young monk sat patiently in the presence of his preceptor waiting for instruction. Eventually, his eagerness exceeded his patience.

"What do I do?"

"What do you do?" echoed his teacher, "What do you need to do?"

An executive met with his meditation teacher.

"How do I know if I'm making progress?" he asked. "How can I tell?"

"Why do you need to know you are making progress?"

Notes

He's still comparing

The comparing mind is one of the last reactive patterns to be released. Traditionally speaking, one is free from the comparing mind only in full awakening (buddhahood). Avalokiteshvara is usually regarded as a ninth level bodhisattva, two levels short of buddhahood.

his three daughters

In the opening scene of Shakespeare's *King Lear*, Lear makes his three daughters compete with each other in professing their love for him. Cordelia, his youngest daughter, refuses to participate and is disinherited.

...the mantra that is equal to the unequalled...

What equals the unequalled?

*The light of the moon falling
On a granite dome,*

*A wisp of spray whisked
From the curl of a wave,*

*One white flower in a sea
Of cherry blossoms*

*The laughter of a child
Running in the sun,*

*The quiet in you
When a friend's tear
Falls on your arm.*

If he keeps flinging around these epithets, people will take him seriously and start to worship it.

What good will that do them?

And he's right on the edge of making something out of nothing.

Better to be on the receiving end of that deal.

The moment you start thinking, the world splits in two.

The moment you try to stop thinking, the world splits in two.

When is the world one?

Notes

Better to be on the receiving end of that deal
From the Mahayana tradition of mind training:
> *Give all gain and victory to others. Take all loss and defeat for yourself.*
> —Langri Tangpa, *Mind Training in Seven Verses*
> *Gain is illusion. Loss is enlightenment.*
> —Uchiyama Roshi, *How to Cook Your Life*

the world splits in two.
> *Make the smallest distinction, however, and heaven and earth are set infinitely apart.*
> —Chien-chih Seng-ts'an, *Verses on the Faith Mind*

...the mantra which completely calms all suffering...

*Imagine a world
Where
The road has no bumps,
The sea no waves,
The fire no sparks,
The wind no gusts,
And the sky no clouds.
What kind of life is that?*

Don't be fooled. He's not talking about the four easy escapes:

> the self-righteous complacency that allows you to dismiss the vicissitudes that afflict your fellow beings,

> the formal courtesy that masks your cruelty with the sterility of social dictates,

> the heartless justice that enables you to impose values on the helpless and unfortunate,

> the celebration of the trivial and the inconsequential that artificially inflates self-esteem.

How do you calm suffering? Stop fighting what you experience.

four easy escapes
Corruptions of the four immeasurables: equanimity, loving kindness, compassion, and joy. The uncorrupted expression of the four immeasurables calms the suffering of others.
See *Wake Up to Your Life*, pg. 244.

...is not a ruse: know it to be true.

*No one can show you
What is true.
That's up to you.*

*All his yammering comes down to this:
Look, and look again,
Until you see nothing,
Inside or out.*

Perhaps he's just another one of those people who shove The Truth in your face.

First it was an opening, then a memory, then an idea. Unnoticed, it became a belief and then an ideology. Now it's a *casus belli*, and you are ready to wreak havoc on all who disagree.

The Truth is its own falsification.

What is true?

Find what is not true, and let it go.

What's left?

That's up to you.
The most that a teacher can do is to help create the conditions in which seeing, the experience of presence, or awakening can arise. The student needs three things: willingness, know-how, and capacity. Willingness involves being willing to let go of the world of projections and to meet whatever arises. It is connected with faith. Know-how means knowing how to cultivate attention, step out of projections, and rest in experience. Know-how can be taught. Capacity means to have a sufficient capacity in attention to be able to use the know-how one develops in practice. Capacity can be developed. Many people don't put enough energy into building capacity. They strive to understand aspects of practice that cannot be understood intellectually, but can be known relatively easily when there is a sufficient capacity in attention.

wreak havoc on all who disagree
   Faced with the choice of changing one's mind and proving there's no need to do so, almost everybody gets busy on the proof.
   — John Kenneth Galbraith (1908 - 2006)

The mantra of the perfection of wisdom is said in this way...

No shape, no color, no eye —
You can't see it.
No tongue, no sound, no ear —
You can't say it.
No idea, no thinking, no mind —
You can't imagine it.
Say it, now, without shape, word, or thought.

Transform objects! Disappear in a crowd! Release the energy in your secret centers! Make your mind one with the universe! Draw nutrition from stones!

Sorcerers have a spell for everything.

But you have to pronounce each syllable correctly.

This didn't stop an old hermit from walking across a lake.

How do you say this mantra?

walking across a lake

A hermit, renowned for his spiritual understanding, lived on an island in the middle of a lake. Two scholars went to visit him. As they rowed across the lake, they saw rainbows surrounding the island. They met with the hermit and asked him about his practice.

"Oh," he said, "I just recite the six-syllable mantra *om mani padme ox.*"

"You mean *om mani padme hung*, don't you, the mantra of Avalokiteshvara?" one of the scholars asked.

"Oh my, have I been reciting it wrong? Thank you for telling me."

The scholars left, but as they rowed away, the hermit came running over the water to catch up to them.

"What was the correct pronunciation?" he asked.

The scholars looked at each other. One of them turned to the old man and replied, "Never mind what we said. What you've been doing is fine."

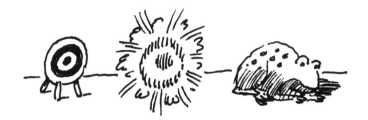

om gaté gaté paragaté parasamgaté bodhi svaha

Earth, sky
As the car wended its way across the plain
We were no longer able to see
Where one started, one stopped, or even where they met.

The effect was...
Startling,
Leaving us
Suspended in space
With no sense of time, direction, or goal.

We drove on without map or guide,
Dealing as best we could
With rutted roads and failing light
Trusting something we could feel, perhaps know,
But could never put in words.

In the end we were completely lost.
We were in the dark, inside and out,
With nothing in between.

That was all a long time ago,
Or was it?
It's hard to tell
Where the past begins and the future ends, or even where they meet.

You can, if you wish, figure out what the mantra means. You won't be the first. Whatever you come up with, put it over there — with all the other dung.

Do you want to know what the mantra means?

Don't quiet what is already quiet. Don't block what can't be blocked. When you walk, don't move. When you talk, say not a word.

_____ Notes

When you walk, don't move
  These moving feet reveal a walker
  But did not start him on his way.
  There was no walker prior to departure
  Who was going where?
    —Stephen Batchelor, *Verses from the Center*

When you talk, say not a word
  A white flower grows in the quiet.
  Let your tongue become that flower.
    — Rumi (1207 - 1273)

Thus, Shariputra, do all bodhisattva mahasattvas
train in the profound perfection of wisdom."

The mighty walls of marble, rock and stone,
The lofty parapets, banners streaming in the air,
The soaring towers gleaming in the sun,
Mere rubble now:
Ground returned to ground.

Clouds drift in an open sky:
No home,
No path,
No aim.

Don't make the mistake of thinking that the old dog has to learn new tricks.

The worst thing he can do now is to toddle after all those great beings and try to join their club. Just ask that mad man with the cigar and moustache.

A rose isn't a violet and a violet isn't a rose. And yet, we enjoy both.

_____ Notes

Mere rubble now
Avalokiteshvara has effectively demolished the edifice the Sarvastivadins built to categorize experience and explain how awakening comes about. While the sutra may be interpreted as a refutation of a particular school of thought, one may also see the sutra as both a refutation of the tendencies in all of us to conceptualize and concretize the essential mystery of this experience we call "life", and a pointing to the experience of presence itself.

the old dog
In the end, the elegant maps constructed by the Sarvastivadins do not put you in touch with natural knowing because they chart things that were never there in the first place. The point of Avalokiteshvara's presentation was to show Shariputra that the effort to understand experience is precisely what prevents one from knowing experience completely.

that mad man with the cigar and moustache
   I don't want to belong to any club that will accept me as a member.
     — Groucho Marx (1890 - 1977)

Confirmation

Then Lord Buddha arose from that absorption and praised noble Avalokiteshvara, the bodhisattva mahasattva, saying, "Well done, well done, o son of noble family; thus it is, thus it is. One experiences the profound perfection of wisdom just as you have taught. Those Who Have Gone This Way also rejoice."

You can tell the character of every man when you see how he receives praise.
— Seneca (5 BCE - 65 CE)

Then Lord Buddha arose from that absorption...

This is not the stillness of death,
That absence of life
When you look upon what is so familiar
And know she is there no more.

Nor is this the stillness of absence,
Emptied of movement,
Where dust quietly suffocates furniture
And nothing stirs the air.

No, this is the stillness of presence,
A peace beyond thought
Where you know you've been asleep
And are free now
From your restless dreams.

The one time I saw the film, I thought the projector had frozen, or I was watching a slide.

In the patchy sunlight that filtered into the temple, he sat on a throne, a black ritual hat crowning his head, utterly still. I felt I was looking into a forest pool, a pool so still and so deep in the forest that nothing, not even a breath of wind, had disturbed it for a thousand years.

As the camera slowly zoomed in, I saw his lips were moving, ever so slightly, and that this person, whom I'd met a number of times, embodied a stillness that went beyond, far beyond, ordinary composure.

When you end a meditation session, where does the stillness go?

  Notes

a stillness that went beyond, far beyond, ordinary composure
My experience when I watched the opening scene with H.H. Karmapa XVI
in Arnaud Desjardin's film *The Message of the Tibetans*.

> ...and praised noble Avalokiteshvara, the bodhisattva mahasattva, saying, "Well done, well done, o son of noble family...

Stubborn ox!
Yesterday a smart slap,
Today a handful of hay.

"Don't expect thanks," Chekawa said. Fair enough.

Seeking praise is one thing. Receiving praise is another.

Some teachers you just can't please.

You bust your ass in practice. You have visions, dreams, and very strange experiences. You tell her about them and ask for help, but all she says is, "Not good, not bad — keep going."

One day, you just know and you don't even bother to ask.

Later she drops by and you tell her.

Now she makes a big fuss.

Meanwhile, you're just sitting there saying nothing.

Some teachers you just can't please.

Notes

Don't expect thanks
The last instruction in Chekawa Yeshe Dorje's *Mind Training in Seven Points*. See *The Great Path of Awakening* by Kongtrul.

Thus it is, thus it is.

You look into his eyes.
He looks into yours.
Whether it's
The beginning, the middle, or the end,
You know
And you know that
He knows,
Too.

What's the big picture, here?

Two points of view:

Things exist! Just follow this path from ignorance to awareness. Here, these maps will help.

Nothing exists, not even ignorance or awareness — and there is no path. What use are your maps?

Buddha supported just one of them. What happened to the middle way?

What do you do?

Chew on this until your teeth fall out. Anything less won't do.

Notes

Things exist

The Sarvastivadin position, which Shariputra represents, sees experience as arising from combinations of elements of experience (dharmas). The ontological status of these elements is not clearly specified, but the Sarvastivadins seem to have regarded them as existing in some sense. In this way, they represent the tendency in all of us to concretize experience and the path to complete awareness. They developed numerous maps (the five groups, the twelve sense-fields, the eighteen elements, the twelve links, the four truths, etc.) to chart this path.

Nothing exists

The perspective of the perfection of wisdom, presented by Avalokiteshvara, categorically denies any ontological status to all aspects of experience, including, of course, all the maps of the Sarvastivadins.

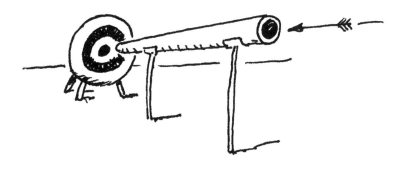

> One experiences the profound perfection of wisdom
> just as you have taught.

*Why pick up rabbit horns in the desert,
Or knit a sweater out of turtle hair?*

*You have to be blind to see this path
And deaf to hear these instructions.*

*Sketch a scene on the side of a wave.
Climb a staircase in a dream.*

If you try to approach it, you move away.

If you try to stay in it, you lose it completely.

If you try to avoid it, you spin in confusion.

Not seeing is seeing.

Not practicing is practicing.

Notes

rabbit horns...turtle hair
Two analogies used in the Perfection of Wisdom sutras to illustrate that no ontological status can be assigned to any aspect of experience.

blind to see this path
Conventional ways of understanding have to be discarded because they are based on subject-object projections.

> *In order to arrive at what you do not know*
> *You must go by a way which is the way of ignorance.*
> —T. S. Eliot, *Four Quartets*

deaf to hear these instructions
The *Heart Sutra*, and similar instructions, cannot be understood with the intellect. One must be deaf to the conceptual articulations and rely on the indefinable experience of knowing itself.

Those Who Have Gone This Way also rejoice."

Blue skies
Smilin' at me
Deep light of the sun
Awake inside me
Ain't it great
Bein' so free
Nothin' but blue skies
Do I see

No theory of competition is complete that doesn't account for the joy some teachers experience when their own students exceed them.

And theories of jealousy must explain the special pleasure felt when you give your favorite childhood toy to your young niece and watch her play.

When others take delight
In giving praise to those endowed with talents,
Why, O mind, do you not find
A joy, likewise, in praising them?
    — Shantideva, *The Way of the Bodhisattva*

Notes

Those Who Have Gone This Way
Skt. *Tathagata*, literally, "those who have gone this way" or "those who have gone to suchness", an epithet for buddhas.

Blue skies
Smilin' at me...
Adapted from the song:
> *Blue skies*
> *Smiling at me*
> *Nothing but blue skies*
> *Do I see*
>   — Irving Berlin, *Blue Skies*, 1927

Conclusion

Then venerable Shariputra and noble Avalokiteshvara,
the bodhisattva mahasattva, that whole assembly and
the world with its gods, humans, titans, and sky spirits,
rejoiced and praised the words of Lord Buddha.

The secret of a good sermon is to have a good beginning and a good ending, then having the two as close together as possible.
— George Burns (1896 - 1996)

Then venerable Shariputra and noble Avalokiteshvara, the bodhisattva mahasattva, that whole assembly and the world with its gods, humans, titans, and sky spirits, rejoiced and praised the words of Lord Buddha.

> *The final accolade!*
> *The curtain descends.*
> *The party is over.*
> *The guests leave, tipping the parking valets,*
> *As they exchange the usual pleasantries,*
> *Leaving behind*
> *Scattered plates of unfinished food and half-empty glasses.*
> *Where will they go?*
> *What will they do?*

It's been a long night and you've probably eaten too much.

If anything rattled you, don't throw up. Let it work in you — until the you that you are now is fatally poisoned. The importance of a conventional life is greatly exaggerated and a good death can do wonders.

Look at this mess! Time to clean up.

Put the leftovers outside for those who couldn't come — because they were confused, lost their way, had better things to do, or were detained by the authorities.

As for the authorities, may the dark forces of compassion, the black weapon-wielding monsters in tiger-skin kilts and elephant-hide shawls, riding rabid bears and demon horses, correct and complete anything I've left undone.

Here is my prayer for you.

> May you never sleep.
> May you never eat.
> May you never go home.
> May you never find a path.

Remember, the reason to know emptiness is to be able to act and rest freely.

How do you act? Let the struggles of others be your guide.

How do you rest? Let the struggles of others be your guide.

Notes

Put the leftovers outside
In the Tibetan tradition, at the end of feast ceremonies (Skt. *ganacakra*, Tib. tshogs kyi 'khor lo), a portion of the leftover food is consecrated and put outside for the demons who couldn't attend the feast. This ritual element can be seen as a way to form a connection with the areas of one's own psyche that are not yet open to awareness.

As for the authorities
The protectors of the Shangpa tradition are the Six-armed Mahakala, Remati and their retinue. Protectors can be seen as the expressions of direct awareness that naturally create conditions for awakening. The protectors represent the way direct awareness knows precisely how to cut through the most intractable patterns of resistance or projection.

correct and complete anything I've left undone
Most Vajrayana ceremonies conclude with a confession of mistakes made in the ceremony and a request to the protectors not to be upset by errors or lapses in attention.

Bibliography

Adams, Douglas
The Restaurant at the End of the Universe
Del Rey, 2005

Batchelor, Stephen
Verses from the Center: A Buddhist Vision of the Sublime
Riverhead Books, 2001

Carroll, Lewis
Alice's Adventures in Wonderland
The Millennium Fulcrum Edition 3.0
www.cs.cmu.edu/~rgs/alice-table.html

Carroll, Lewis
Through the Looking Glass
The Millennium Fulcrum Edition 1.7
www.jus.uio.no/sisu/through_the_looking_glass.lewis_carroll/2.html

Chekawa Yeshe Dorje
Mind Training in Seven Points
Translation by Ken McLeod
Unfettered Mind www.unfetteredmind.org

Chogyam Trungpa
Illusion's Game: The Life and Teaching of Naropa
Shambhala Publications, 2004

Guenther, Herbert V.
The Life and Teaching of Naropa
Shambhala Publications, 2004

Hakuin
Zen Words for the Heart: Hakuin's Commentary on the Heart Sutra
Translated by Norman Waddell, Shambhala, 1996

Hopkins, Jeffrey
Meditations on Emptiness
Wisdom Publications, 1996

Jamgön Kongtrul
The Great Path of Awakening: The Classic Guide to Lojong, a Tibetan Buddhist Practice for Cultivating the Heart of Compassion
Translated by Ken McLeod, Shambhala Publications, 2005

Jigme Lingpa
The Wisdom Experience of Ever-present Good
Translation by Ken McLeod, Unpublished manuscript.

Kyer-gong-pa
Recognizing Your Mind as the Guru
Translation by Ken McLeod
Unfettered Mind www.unfetteredmind.org

Lopez, Donald S, Jr.
The Heart Sutra Explained
South Asia Books, 1990

McLeod, Ken
Wake Up to Your Life: Discovering the Buddhist Path of Attention
Harper San Francisco, 2002

Merton, Thomas
The Way of Chuang Tzu
Shambhala Publications, 2004

Milarepa
The Hundred Thousand Songs of Milarepa
Translated by Garma C. C. Chang, University Books, 1962

Rangjung Dorje
Aspirations for Mahamudra
Translation by Ken McLeod
Unfettered Mind www.unfetteredmind.org

Red Pine
The Heart Sutra: the Womb of Buddhas
Shoemaker & Hoard, 2004

Riggs, Nicole
Like an Illusion: Lives of the Shangpa Kagyu Masters
Dharma Cloud Publishers, 2000

Ryokan
One Robe, One Bowl: The Zen Poetry of Ryokan
Translated by John Stevens, Weatherhill, 2006

Shah, Idries
Tales of the Dervishes
The Octagon Press, 1993

Uchiyama, Kosho
How to Cook Your Life: From the Zen Kitchen to Enlightenment
Shambhala Publications, 2005

Wittgenstein, Ludwig
Tractatus Logico Philosophicus

ISBN 142513377-0

Made in the USA
Lexington, KY
19 September 2012